I LOVE
NIALL
Are you his ultimate fan?

Written by Jen Wainwright

Edited by Bryony Jones
Design by Barbara Ward
Cover design by Zoe Bradley

Picture Acknowledgements:
Front cover: Stuart Wilson/Getty Images
Back cover: Michael Buckner/WireImage/Getty Images
Picture section:
Page 1, Matt Baron/BEI/Rex Features
Page 2, David Thompson/Rex Features
Page 3, Slaven Vlasic/Getty Images
Page 4, Matt Baron/BEI/Rex Features
Page 5, Picture Perfect/Rex Features
Pages 6–7, Ian West/PA Wire/Press Association Images
Page 8, Veda Jo Jenkins/Rex Features

First published in Great Britain in 2013 by Buster Books,
an imprint of Michael O'Mara Books Limited, 9 Lion Yard, Tremadoc Road,
London SW4 7NQ

www.busterbooks.co.uk

Text copyright © Buster Books 2013

Artwork adapted from www.shutterstock.com

A CIP catalogue record for this book is available from the British Library.

ISBN: 978-1-78055-216-3

PLEASE NOTE: This book is not affiliated with or endorsed by One Direction or
any of their publishers or licensees.

10 9 8 7 6 5 4 3 2 1

Printed and bound in February 2013 by CPI Group (UK) Ltd, 108 Beddington Lane,
Croydon, CR0 4YY, United Kingdom.

Papers used by Buster Books are natural, recyclable products made from wood
grown in sustainable forests. The manufacturing processes conform to the
environmental regulations of the country of origin.

I LOVE
NIALL
Are you his ultimate fan?

Buster Books

Contents

About this book

One Direction are five of your favourite people in the world. You know all their songs by heart, there are posters of them on your walls, and you're bursting with pride every time they achieve something new and spectacular.

But there's one member of the band who you love more than all the others – it's the Irish cutie Niall Horan.

It's time to find out just how much you know about your fave 1D lad. This book is full of super-fun quizzes and totally tricky trivia for you to test your Niall knowledge. There are also games to play with your friends, stories to complete, horoscopes, puzzles and much more, plus some gorgeous, glossy pics of Niall for you to gaze at.

What are you waiting for? Dive in, and test your super fan status.

It's phenomeNiall!

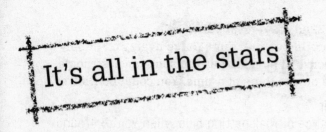

It's all in the stars

DISCOVER WHAT YOUR STAR SIGN REVEALS
ABOUT YOU, THEN FIND OUT WHAT PART YOU
COULD PLAY IN NIALL'S LIFE.

★ ARIES (21st March – 20th April) ★

You've got the makings of a real leader. You're great at
making decisions and rarely feel stressed by being under
pressure. You can sometimes act on impulse and you don't
like to be told you're in the wrong. You could be Niall's:

Manager

You'd be fab at organizing the packed schedule of the
biggest band on the planet, and planning the best tour ever
to keep Directioners happy.

★ TAURUS (21st April – 21st May) ★

Patient and understanding, you're a loyal friend who never
gives up when faced with a problem. You can be a bit of a
shopaholic and you love treating yourself to tasty meals out
and nice new things. You could be Niall's:

Personal chef

You and Niall share a love of good food, so you're the
perfect person to whip up some delicious snacks after a
long day of rehearsals.

GEMINI (22nd May – 21st June)

You're all about the fun, fun, fun! You're lively and bubbly with a great sense of humour, but you sometimes struggle to concentrate on one thing at a time. You could be Niall's:

Morale booster

There's no chance of Niall getting blue when you're around. Your positive attitude and amazing energy will have him feeling happy in no time.

CANCER (22nd June– 23rd July) ★

Quiet and clever, you're brilliant at finding solutions to problems. You love to make others feel confident, but you can get a little bit moody if things don't go your way. You could be Niall's:

Interviewer

With your intuition and cool, questioning mind, you're sure to have the skills to discover Niall's biggest secrets.

★ LEO (24th July – 23rd August) ★

You're artistic and creative, and you love to get hands-on with any project that comes your way. You can sometimes be a bit on the bossy side, but you're so loveable that you get away with it! You could be Niall's:

Stylist

Your vision and creativity make you an ideal person to ensure Niall's always looking his most gorgeous best.

VIRGO (24th August – 23rd September)

You're a great listener and you care about your friends. You're a multi-talented person who wants to make sure that everything you turn your hand to is the best it can be. You could be Niall's:

Perfect match

The gorgeous Mr Horan is a Virgo, too. You both strive for perfection, which makes you perfect for each other.

LIBRA (24th September – 23rd October)

You've got the ability to charm the socks off anyone you meet. You're talkative and intelligent, and you always look on the bright side of life. You could be Niall's:

Publicist

Just in case anyone needs persuading about Niall's cuteness, talent and super-sweet personality – you're the person for the job!

SCORPIO (24th October – 22nd November)

There's a real spark in you. You're determined and talented, and you can achieve anything you put your mind to, no matter how tricky it may be. You could be Niall's:

Personal trainer

You're a bit of a firecracker who'd provide Niall with some healthy competition, and keep him on his toes. He would want to pull out all the stops to impress you.

SAGITTARIUS (23rd November – 21st December)

You're a gentle free spirit who hates to be tied down. You're happiest in the great outdoors, and you love trying new experiences. You could be Niall's:

Tour buddy

Your love of travel and infectious grin will keep Niall feeling excited about every new place he visits, even when he's really tired.

★ CAPRICORN (22nd December – 20th January)

Reliable and organized, you're a practical person who keeps calm in a crisis. You could be Niall's:

Assistant

As his trusted assistant and adviser, it's up to you to make sure Niall's where he needs to be. Your role in his life means you get to spend loads of time with him — you lucky thing!

★ AQUARIUS (21st January – 19th February)

You're independent and protective of the people you love, and you're never afraid to stand up for what you believe in. You have a sharp wit, but you can sometimes be quite stubborn. You could be Niall's:

Bodyguard

You'd be the perfect person to protect your fave lad when 1D mania gets a little too crazy.

★ PISCES (20th February – 20th March)

You can be very shy around new people or situations, but you're a faithful friend. You have a powerful imagination and love to daydream. You could be Niall's:

Songwriting partner

With your creative spirit, you and Niall have a lot in common. You'd be great at helping to inspire him and creating future smash hits together.

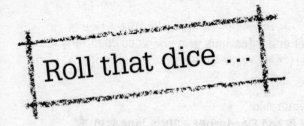

Roll that dice ...

GET READY TO DISCOVER YOUR DESTINY WITH NIALL.
GRAB A DICE AND FOLLOW THE INSTRUCTIONS BELOW TO
SEE INTO THE FUTURE.

1. Come up with your own ideas for categories A to E,
and write them in the 'Your choice' section for each
category.

2. Roll that dice! Roll it once for each of the categories.
The number you roll is the choice that the dice has
made for you.

3. Write down your future with Niall in the box on the
opposite page, and wait to see if it comes true.

CATEGORIES

A. Where you and Niall will meet:
1. At the cinema **2.** At a football match **3.** On the beach
4. At a concert **5.** Outside your school

6. (Your choice) ....

B. What you will do together:
1. Have a tasty picnic **2.** Spend a day at the fun fair

3. Eat lunch at a fancy restaurant **4.** Get competitive at go-karting **5.** Play video games

6. (Your choice) ....

C. He will think you're so:
1. Cute **2.** Funny **3.** Clever **4.** Amazing **5.** Beautiful

6. (Your choice) ....

D. What he will give you as a gift:
1. A song he's written for you **2.** A signed T-shirt
3. A locket with both your pics in **4.** Tickets to his show
5. A red rose

6. (Your choice) ....

E. Where you and Niall will go:
1. New York City **2.** A tropical island **3.** Australia
4. Ireland **5.** London

6. (Your choice) ....

Your future with Niall:

I'm going to meet Niall ....

Together, we will ....

He will think I am ....

As a present, he will give me ....

We'll travel to ....

What's your theme song?

Start
Your BFF is feeling down in the dumps. How are you going to cheer her up?

Make her a photo album showing the fun things you've done together.

It's Saturday and you're heading to the shops. What are you looking for?

1D's new album, and some cool DVDs to watch with your mates at the next sleepover.

Something with a bit of sparkle so you can dazzle at the next party.

Gather all her mates together for a surprise party.

1D's new song comes on the radio. How do you react?

Immediately hit the floor and bust out your best dance moves.

Listen to the lyrics and learn them off by heart ready to sing along next time.

Argh! You fall over in front of your whole class. What do you do next?

→ Blush bright red and run away cringing. →

'Gotta Be You'
You can sometimes be a little bit shy and sensitive. 'Gotta Be You', with it's soulful lyrics and soaring harmonies, never fails to tug at your heartstrings. It's your perfect theme song.

→ Style it out and make it look like it was on purpose. →

'Live While We're Young'
You just love to dance and jump around. The catchy chorus of 'Live While We're Young', and its carefree message, sum up the way you want to live your life.

What time of year makes you the happiest?

→ Summertime. You love fun in the sun and relaxing at the beach. →

→ Winter, snuggled up with hot chocolate by the fire – bliss! →

'Little Things'
If ever you're feeling a little bit blue, putting this song on is sure to make you feel better. All five lads sound amazing in their solos, and the lyrics are so sweet it's like getting a big, warm One Direction hug. Aww!

→ Cutted and in need of a hug and some serious TLC. →

Your crush has a new girlfriend. How do you feel?

→ Just fine. You're glad he's happy, and you'll have more time to be with your BFFs. →

'What Makes You Beautiful'
It's the original 1D anthem, and for you it's the best. You love this song for its upbeat sound and the memories it brings back of One Direction as they were just starting out.

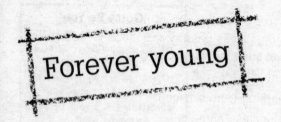

Forever young

SINCE HE SHOT TO SUPERSTARDOM IN ONE DIRECTION, YOU'VE BEEN FOLLOWING NIALL'S EVERY MOVE. BUT HOW MUCH DO YOU KNOW ABOUT HIS LIFE BEFORE HE WAS FAMOUS? TAKE THIS QUIZ TO FIND OUT AND CHECK YOUR ANSWERS ON **PAGE 91**.

1. Where was Niall born?
   a. Dublin
   b. Mullingar
   c. Cork

2. How was Niall's singing talent first discovered by his family?
   a. On a car journey
   b. Hearing him singing in the shower
   c. Watching him on stage at school

3. What is the name of Niall's brother?
   a. Graham
   b. George
   c. Greg

4. He looks like butter wouldn't melt in his mouth, but Niall was a bit of a cheeky chappy at school. Which of his antics got him suspended for two days?

a. Mooning the headteacher

b. Stealing something from a friend

c. Doodling on the classroom wall

5. What does Niall say was the best Christmas present he was ever given as a child?

a. A guitar

b. A Power Rangers toy

c. A remote-control car

6. Niall played the lead in a musical at his primary school. What was the name of the show?

a. *Guys and Dolls*

b *Oliver!*

c. *Grease*

7. Niall went to live with his dad after his parents split up. What's his dad's job?

a. Fireman

b Butcher

c. Baker

8. What sort of music did Niall love listening to when he was younger?

a. Rap

b. Rock

c. Swing

9. Niall has a real fear of birds, but where did this phobia come from?

   a. He was pecked by a sparrow in the park

   b. A bird got its claws caught in his hair

   c. A pigeon flew in his bathroom window when he was on the toilet

10. What was the first live concert that Niall went to?

   a. Busted

   b. Beyoncé

   c. The Backstreet Boys

11. Niall's best mate joined him and the other 1D boys while they were in New York for a few days' downtime. What is his name?

   a. Shane Cullen

   b. Sean Crillen

   c. Sean Cullen

12. Which former *X Factor* contestant did Niall perform with as a support act before he auditioned himself?

   a. Lucie Jones

   b. Lloyd Daniels

   c. Eoghan Quigg

Tweet treats

IN CASE YOU EVER NEED REMINDING OF HOW MUCH NIALL
LOVES HIS FANS, READ THE HEARTFELT TWEETS BELOW
AND GET READY TO FEEL ALL WARM AND FUZZY.

Wooowwwwww! Madrid! The most amazing scenes I've seen! Spanish fans are locoooo! Muchas gracias!

Love the way you trend Morning Nialler every morning! Thank you

As I always say ! Best fans on the planet! Without a doubt!

Was incredible to be at xfactor last night! So strange watching it from the audience! Thank you soo much for everything you've done for us

Thank you all soo much for comin out to see us today! And camping for days in the cold! Dedication from our fans is incredible

Ok! Night everyone!love you all, and thank you for everything you do for us! We love you lots! Mwah xx

Can't believe the itunes charts around the world! Love u guys sooo much ! Smashing it up for us! Glad you're enjoying the album

Would you rather?

IMAGINE YOU'VE GOT THE CHANCE TO SPEND SOME
QUALITY TIME WITH NIALL. WHAT WOULD YOU RATHER
DO? READ THE OPTIONS BELOW AND CHOOSE WHICH
OPTION YOU'D PREFER.

Would you rather ...

Hang out with Niall for
a day? 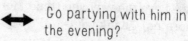 Go partying with him in
the evening?

Get his autograph? 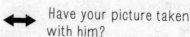 Have your picture taken
with him?

Be in the front row at a
1D concert? 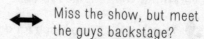 Miss the show, but meet
the guys backstage?

Be Niall's date for a
red-carpet event? Have a private date, just
the two of you?

Learn to do impressions like Niall?  Learn to play guitar like Niall?

Have him follow you on Twitter? 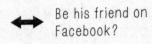 Be his friend on Facebook?

Sing a duet with Niall? 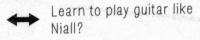 Have him serenade you?

Cook dinner for him?  Have him cook for you?

Style Niall's hair? 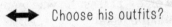 Choose his outfits?

Play a prank on Louis together? 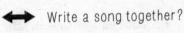 Write a song together?

Show him around your home town? Visit Mullingar with him?

Cringe!

HERE IS PROOF THAT EVEN INTERNATIONAL SUPERSTARS
HAVE EMBARRASSING MOMENTS. READ THE STORIES
BELOW THAT LEFT NIALL RED-FACED, AND DECIDE
WHETHER THEY'RE A TRUE CRINGE, OR A FAKE FAIL.
YOU CAN CHECK YOUR ANSWERS ON **PAGE 91**.

1. Niall was left with a very red face when band mate
Louis pulled down his trousers at a motorway
service station in front of loads of people! While it
was embarrassing, Niall says it could have been
worse – at least he was wearing a nice pair of Calvin
Klein boxers!

☐ True Cringe   ☐ Fake Fail

2. He's got no shortage of admirers nowadays, but Niall's
first kiss was not a success. He says it was so bad that
he's actually blocked it from his memory!

☐ True Cringe   ☐ Fake Fail

3. While Niall was on tour in the USA, he had a
nightmare so terrifying that he wouldn't eat chicken
for the next three weeks. He screamed so loud that
he woke up the rest of the band mates. A hotel porter

even knocked on the door to check that everything was okay. Niall didn't dare answer in case it was the evil giant chicken from his dream!

☐ True Cringe   ☐ Fake Fail

4. Niall's fashion sense hasn't always been as sharp as it is today. When he was 11 years old, he had a 'V' shape shaved into the back of his head. While he was happy with it at the time, he now looks back and thinks it looked 'disgusting'.

☐ True Cringe   ☐ Fake Fail

5. Niall likes to put bubble-bath foam on his face to see what he would look like with a big, bushy beard. He once forgot that he had it on his face and went to do some shopping, looking a bit like Father Christmas!

☐ True Cringe   ☐ Fake Fail

6. Niall had a disaster on the golf course when his trousers split! He bent down to tie his shoelaces on the first hole and there was a horrible ripping sound and a sudden breeze around his bottom. Whoops!

☐ True Cringe   ☐ Fake Fail

7. When on tour, the boys play lots of different cities in super-quick time, which can get confusing. Niall once excitedly shouted, 'London, make some noise!' to the crowd … the only problem was that they were in Berlin!

☐ True Cringe   ☐ Fake Fail

What was the question?

IT'S TIME TO TURN AN INTERVIEW ON ITS HEAD! MATCH THE ANSWERS GIVEN BY NIALL IN INTERVIEWS TO THE QUESTIONS THEY REFER TO. BEWARE, THERE ARE MORE QUESTIONS THAN ANSWERS, SO THINK CAREFULLY. YOU CAN CHECK YOUR ANSWERS ON **PAGE 91**.

Niall's Answers:

1. 'I'd give up, cos I'd get too hungry early.'

2. 'Yes. Louis doesn't though, Louis is the only one that doesn't.'

3. 'Homer Simpson'

4. 'I'd build a big shed, like a massive garage thing.'

5. 'We want to see more of them.'

6. 'I just haven't got around to it yet. I'm very busy at the moment. Maybe when we finish off the album. Maybe around Christmas time.'

7. 'The night of my birthday.'

Questions:

A. When was the last time you pulled an all-nighter?

B. Why haven't you asked me to marry you yet?

C. What would be your strategy to survive *The Hunger Games*?

D. What's been the most typically celeb evening you've had?

E. When do you think you will take your driving test?

F. Do you take sugar in your tea?

G. If you had to be a cartoon, who would you be?

H. What do you think of boy fans?

I. What fictional character would be your best friend?

J. Do you love going out and partying on your days off?

K. If I gave you an elephant, where would you hide it?

Write your answers here:

1. ....

2. ....

3. ....

4. ....

5. ....

6. ....

7. ....

All directions!

CAN YOU FIND THE WORDS LISTED BELOW THAT ARE
HIDDEN IN THE GRID ON THE PAGE OPPOSITE? ALL OF
THE WORDS ARE CONNECTED TO NIALL AND HIS WORLD.
THEY COULD BE HIDDEN FORWARDS, BACKWARDS,
UPWARDS, DOWNWARDS OR EVEN DIAGONALLY.
YOU CAN FIND THE ANSWERS ON **PAGE 92**.

NIALL	UP ALL NIGHT
HARRY	NANDOS
LIAM	MULLINGAR
LOUIS	SIMON COWELL
ZAYN	TAKE ME HOME

L	L	E	W	O	C	N	O	M	I	S	L	B	W	T
L	P	A	Y	B	A	Z	S	T	I	A	L	O	U	K
A	Q	U	E	Z	Y	N	W	L	G	O	A	O	M	R
I	S	R	A	G	N	I	L	L	U	M	A	N	I	E
N	Y	A	Z	L	M	M	O	I	J	T	H	W	A	I
H	T	C	K	O	S	T	S	O	P	A	R	N	R	N
J	J	R	A	O	E	H	E	E	N	K	P	A	K	E
O	L	Y	D	I	A	G	R	R	Y	E	M	U	O	L
E	D	N	B	D	D	I	F	R	O	M	A	S	T	H
L	A	R	H	I	Q	N	I	K	W	E	L	I	A	M
N	H	H	T	A	K	L	U	P	A	H	Y	R	O	O
Y	G	A	R	O	G	L	P	E	E	O	G	T	B	E
N	O	R	U	S	H	A	T	H	E	M	H	S	I	M
O	X	R	W	A	B	P	T	U	P	E	T	L	L	O
Z	A	Y	B	M	O	U	L	E	X	T	A	L	E	O

Stole my heart

NIALL IS KNOWN AS 'THE CUTE ONE' OF THE BAND — AND
WITH GOOD REASON. THE STORIES BELOW ARE SURE TO
MAKE YOUR HEART MELT. USE THE CUTE-O-METER
TO GIVE EACH ONE A RATING, BY COLOURING IN THE
HEARTS UNDER EACH STORY.

Cute-O-Meter

 Aww

 What A Cutie!

 Super Sweet

 Cuteness Overload

 I Can't Even Cope With
How Cute This Is!

Niall recorded a special message for a young American fan on her 16th birthday. Melena Butera, who has Down's Syndrome, made a film for the band with her older sister, explaining what a huge fan she was. Niall was touched by the film and sent a personal message back to Melena, calling her 'absolutely incredible', sending love from all the boys and blowing her a kiss at the end.

Down-to-earth Niall is never afraid to give back to people less fortunate than himself. Rather than spending his 19th birthday opening presents, eating chocolate, being spoilt rotten and blowing out lots of candles, Niall chose to host not one but two incredible events to raise money for autism and emergency-housing charities.

Part of the fundraiser involved a wonderful round of golf in Westmeath and attracted a lot of attention from fans and sports lovers alike. There was such a rush for tickets to the event that the website crashed!

The entire band is always keen to do more charity work. In October 2012, for example, One Direction took a break from their busy schedules to go and visit seriously ill children in London. The charity, called Rays Of Sunshine, helps grant exciting wishes for young kids. The boys played games, answered questions, signed autographs, posed for photos and ran a few errands, including 'biscuit fetching'. Niall spoke for the whole of 1D when he said, 'It is totally humbling to meet kids like this. And it really makes you feel good that you can do something nice for them. We've had amazing good luck, and many of these children haven't. But they are always happy and we go away feeling brilliant. It's like we're giving something back.'

Niall is a self-confessed Twitter addict. His tweets are sometimes sweet and sometimes super funny, but he recently took to the micro blogging site to show his caring, protective side, as he expressed his concern for his New York fans' safety. He wrote: 'Guys u gotta stay safe please!I beg you! Don't chase after cars and stuff ! This is manhattan we're talkin, busy streets' ... 'I don't want anyone gettin hurt! Please stay safe!'

Niall and the rest of the boys helped raise £50,000 for Flying Start (British Airways's charity partnership with Comic Relief) as they took to the skies in the specially named BA1D. The plane was crammed full of adoring fans who all got to spend some quality time with the band.

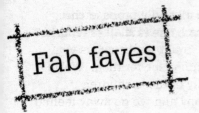

NIALL'S YOUR FAVOURITE GUY, BUT HOW MUCH DO YOU KNOW ABOUT THE STUFF HE LOVES? TAKE THIS QUIZ TO FIND OUT ABOUT A FEW OF HIS FAVOURITE THINGS. YOU CAN CHECK YOUR ANSWERS ON **PAGE 92**.

1. Which of these superb singers is Niall's favourite?
   a. Elton John
   b. Michael Bublé
   c. Michael Jackson

2. Sports-mad Niall is a big football fan, but which team does he support?
   a. Newcastle United
   b. Liverpool
   c. Derby County

3. If Nialler could be any character from a movie, who would he be?
   a. Sebastian from *The Little Mermaid*
   b. Danny Zuko from *Grease*
   c. Edward Cullen from *Twilight*

4. Niall and the other boys are all really proud of the songs they've made, but which one is Niall's favourite?

a. 'One Thing'

b. 'Gotta Be You'

c. 'C'mon, C'mon'

5. It's no secret that Niall loves eating at Nando's, but how spicy does he like his chicken to be?

a. Medium

b. Extra hot

c. Mild

6. What is Nialler's favourite animal?

a. A lion

b. A pigeon

c. A giraffe

7. You know he's a colourful character, but what's his favourite colour?

a. Red

b. Green

c. Black

8. One of the best things about being in One Direction is the amazing places the boys get to visit. Where did Niall say was his fave place?

a. New Zealand

b. Sweden

c. Italy

9. Niall loves a real mix of music, from swing to classic rock, but what's his favourite track of all time?

a. 'Viva La Vida' by Coldplay

b. 'Don't Stop Me Now' by Queen

c. 'One Time' by Justin Bieber

10. The One Direction boys are all really hard workers, and their time off is precious to them. What's Niall's fave thing to do on his days off?

a. Play sport

b. Chill out in front of the TV

c. Have a massive party with his mates

11. To you, he's the cutest star there is, but which of these celebs does Niall have a bit of a crush on?

a. Rihanna

b. Keira Knightley

c. Demi Lovato

12. Niall likes to make sure he smells good at all times. What's his favourite aftershave?

a. Calvin Klein's CK One

b. Georgio Armani's Mania

c. Hugo Boss's Boss Orange.

Dream date with Niall

Start
You're off on holiday. What's your dream destination?

A new and exciting city, with bright lights, great shops and delicious food.

What's the first thing you do when you arrive?

Chill out at your posh hotel and get used to your new surroundings.

Read the guidebook and make a list of the places you want to visit.

A remote beach in the sun where you can lie back and relax.

What three must-have items have you packed?

A camera, some suncream and some holiday reading.

Two bright bikinis and your coolest shades.

I ♥ NIALL

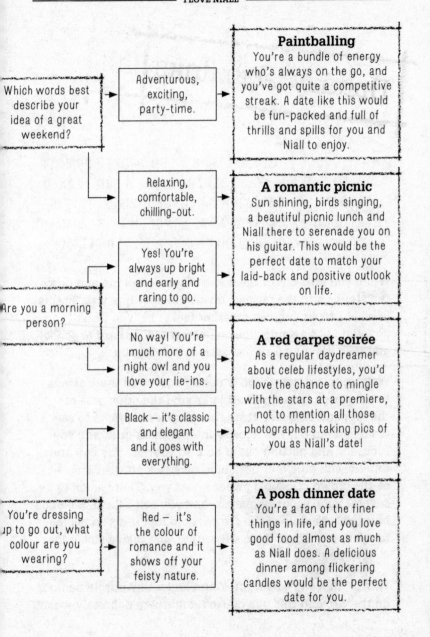

Which words best describe your idea of a great weekend?

Adventurous, exciting, party-time.

Paintballing
You're a bundle of energy who's always on the go, and you've got quite a competitive streak. A date like this would be fun-packed and full of thrills and spills for you and Niall to enjoy.

Relaxing, comfortable, chilling-out.

A romantic picnic
Sun shining, birds singing, a beautiful picnic lunch and Niall there to serenade you on his guitar. This would be the perfect date to match your laid-back and positive outlook on life.

Yes! You're always up bright and early and raring to go.

Are you a morning person?

No way! You're much more of a night owl and you love your lie-ins.

A red carpet soirée
As a regular daydreamer about celeb lifestyles, you'd love the chance to mingle with the stars at a premiere, not to mention all those photographers taking pics of you as Niall's date!

Black – it's classic and elegant and it goes with everything.

You're dressing up to go out, what colour are you wearing?

Red – it's the colour of romance and it shows off your feisty nature.

A posh dinner date
You're a fan of the finer things in life, and you love good food almost as much as Niall does. A delicious dinner among flickering candles would be the perfect date for you.

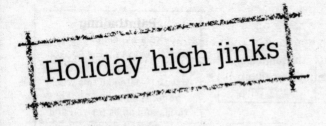

Holiday high jinks

WHAT COULD BE BETTER THAN A FUN-PACKED SUMMER
HOLIDAY TO AN EXOTIC DESTINATION? A FUN-PACKED
SUMMER HOLIDAY WITH NIALL, OF COURSE! THIS IS
YOUR CHANCE TO TAKE CENTRE STAGE IN THIS SUMMERY
STORY – WHAT WILL HAPPEN NEXT? YOU DECIDE!

When you step out of the doors of the aeroplane and down
the steps on to the tarmac, a wave of heat hits you. So this
is what proper summer weather feels like, you think to
yourself with a smile. You've been studying hard at school
and now it's time for some serious holiday fun.

Waiting to get your bags is taking ages, and there seems
to be a large crowd gathering around the other side of
the luggage carousel. Even though you're curious to see
what's going on, you're more interested in grabbing your
rucksack and getting out of here so your holiday can start!
Finally, you pull your dark blue rucksack off the carousel,
as the crowd of people sweeps past you. There seem to be
several huge security guards, and you see a flash of blonde
hair in the middle of the crowd. I wonder if it's someone
famous, you think, then, shrugging, you take a closer look
at your bag.

Wait … this can't be right. Yours had a tiny purple padlock
on the zip, and this one doesn't, and there definitely wasn't

this shamrock sticker on it when you gave it in at the airport. When you look at the name on the tag, you nearly pass out. OMG, this is Niall Horan's bag! And if you've got his, then he must have yours!

If you decide:

1. To chase after Niall and the security guards, go to **A** below.

2. To go through Niall's bag and find out where he's staying, go to **B**, on **page 41**.

A: You spot two girls holding 'I Heart Niall' signs, and they point you in the direction the superstar has gone.

'You'll have to be quick,' says one, 'he was heading for the car – no one knows where he's staying while he's here, we've been trying to find out online but it's all a secret.'

'Thanks,' you say breathlessly, and sprint off in the direction of the rank of cars. Niall's standing by a black limo talking to one of the security guys. You have to take a moment – you can't quite believe you're looking at Niall Horan! In real life! He's wearing a white T-shirt and jeans with some cool shades, and he looks just as cute as he does in the posters on your wall.

You take two steps towards the car and hold up the bag. 'Niall,' you call out, offering your best smile, 'there's been a bit of a mix-up.'

Before you can say anything else, a huge hand clamps down on your shoulder. It's Niall's security man – he really is the biggest guy you've ever seen.

'Niall needs to be leaving now, miss,' he says, giving you a hard stare. 'Time to be moving along.'

'No, no, you don't understand. I'm not a fan … well … I mean, I am a fan, of course I am, it's just …' you realize you're babbling and slow down. 'I've got Niall's bag, and I'm pretty sure he's got mine, look!' You hold up the bag to the security giant. He folds his arms across his enormous chest. 'Prove it,' he says.

If you decide:

1. To tell Niall to open the bag he's got and pull out your beloved toy rabbit, go to **A1**, below.

2. To try and push past the security guard to swap bags with Niall, go to **A2**, on **page 37**.

A1: As you call Niall's name again, his head snaps round to look at you, and you feel yourself going a little bit weak at the knees as your eyes meet.

'What is it?' he asks.

'Just open the bag, please, and hold up the first thing you find in there.'

Niall looks questioningly at the security man, who still has his hand tightly on your shoulder. The big guy nods, and Niall opens the bag. He looks surprised for a second, then he bursts out laughing.

'What on earth is this?' he says, pulling out a giant, fluffy rabbit with floppy ears.

'That's Flopsy, and she's very pleased to meet you,' you say with a grin, looking cheekily up at the security guy, who blushes and lets you go. Niall jogs round the side of the car and comes to greet you.

'I wouldn't dream of kidnapping Flopsy,' he says, handing your bag back to you with a michievous glint in his blue eyes.

'I know, it's a bit lame, but I've had her since I was born and she comes with me everywhere.'

'It's not lame, it's cute,' says Niall. 'You've really saved my skin there. The T-shirt I'm supposed to wear on stage tonight is in that bag – my stylist would have killed me!' He laughs and gives you a hug. 'How can I thank you? I've got some free time this afternoon before the show. Why don't we hang out? We could go to the beach, or if you like I'll find out what the other lads are doing ...'

If you decide:

1. To go with Niall to the beach, go to **A1a**, on **page 39**.

2. To hang out with the rest of the band, go to **A1b**, on **page 39**.

A2: You put your head down, and try to make a run for it past the security guy. You slip past him, but he grabs on to the bag and all of a sudden there's a tug of war situation going on. This wasn't the plan!

Suddenly, there's a horrible ripping sound, and the bag splits along the bottom.

Oh no! You're left holding a shredded bit of material. Niall's stuff is all over the floor, and the security man has a face like thunder. Quickly, you get down on your hands and knees and start trying to gather up as many of Niall's scattered belongings as you can. Your face is glowing bright red with embarrassment and you'd quite like the ground to open up and swallow you whole.

Someone clears their throat, and you're certain you're about to get a serious telling-off. You nervously raise your head, and find yourself staring right into Niall's eyes. He doesn't look angry, in fact, he's trying very hard not to laugh.

'I never liked that bag much anyway,' he says with a chuckle. 'You've just given me an excuse to go shopping – so thanks!'

You smile with relief.

'Seriously though, I owe you one. The boys would never have let me live it down if I'd come to the hotel with a load of girl stuff! I think you've earned a reward. As all my things are so beautifully spread out on the floor for you to see, why don't you pick something to keep as a souvenir?'

If you decide:

1. To take Niall's baseball cap, go to **A2a**, on **page 40**.

2. To take Niall's hotel check-in details, go to **A2b**, on **page 40**.

A1a: The sand is warm between your toes as you kick off your shoes on the beach. You and Niall roll up your jeans and walk through the edge of the waves, chatting and laughing.

Niall's got such a brilliant sense of humour, you feel like you've known him for ages, and you don't want this day to end. After a cut-throat sandcastle-building competition, which you think you won and he thinks he won, Niall looks at his watch.

'Yikes! I've got to go or I'm going to be late for our sound-check.' He leans over and gives you a kiss on the cheek, before running off across the sand. Seconds later, he's back again. 'You should come watch. The show's full tonight but come to the sound-check and I'll introduce you to the others.' He offers you his hand, and together you head across the beach. It's only the first day, and already this is the best holiday ever!

THE END

A1b: Niall makes some calls on his mobile, then beckons to you to get in the car.

'The lads are already at the hotel. Apparently it's got a really cool games arcade,' he says. You gaze out of the window at the scenery flashing past. It's the first time you've been in a car with tinted windows and you feel like a real celebrity. As you pull up to the hotel, the other four 1D boys are there to greet you with big hugs and smiles.

Niall gives you his hand, and your heart is fluttering as you head through the hotel to the games arcade. There are tons of cool machines to play on, and you even manage to beat the boys at a couple of them. It's high fives all round, and you're having the best afternoon of your life!

THE END

A2a: Niall picks up his green cap and puts it gently on your head. 'It suits you,' he says with a grin, 'but there's a little something missing.' Whipping the cap off your head, he pulls out a pen and writes you a message across the brim of the cap.

'There,' he says. 'Perfect.' The message says: 'Hey there. Have bags of fun on your holiday! Lots of love, Niall xxx'.

You laugh and give Niall a hug. 'Thanks, I love it!'

'You should wear it tonight,' he says. 'I'll get you front-row seats at our show, and that way I won't lose your face in the crowd.'

As the concert starts later that night, the crowd goes wild when Niall dedicates the next song to his new, bag-destroying friend. You've never smiled so much in your life!

THE END

A2b: As you read through Niall's hotel details, you hear him chuckling.

'She's a cheeky one, that's for sure,' says the security man, with a stern look on his face.

'I won't keep them, I promise,' you say hurriedly, 'I just wanted to find out where you were staying. It's just down the road from my hotel, and I thought maybe we could hang out or something. Spending some more time with you would be the best souvenir ever!'

The security man's expression softens, and Niall puts an arm around your shoulders. 'Well,' he whispers, 'I think we're planning to get some pizza and chill out before the show tonight. Why not come and join us?'

You nod and give him a hug. You're feeling so happy you even give the security man a hug! No school and an afternoon of pizza with One Direction – perfect!

THE END

B: You unzip the bag and hunt around inside. There's a green baseball cap, a couple of T-shirts, a packet of crisps and – bingo! – an important-looking folder of documents.

You skim through the information on the first sheet and then it hits you – Niall and the rest of the band are staying at your hotel! There's no time to lose, you hail a taxi and drive to the hotel as fast as you can.

When you explain to the lady at the front desk that you've got Niall Horan's bag and that you'd like to go to his room to give it back to him, she just laughs.

'Nice try,' she says, 'but that room number is confidential.' Sighing, you decide to keep the bag with you in case you spot Niall, and explore the hotel. Where do you go first?

If you decide:

1. To head to the pool, go to **B1**, on **page 42**.

2. To check out the restaurant, go to **B2**, on **page 42**.

B1: The pool is huge, and the water looks wonderfully cool and refreshing. All along one end there are twisting waterslides and flumes that look super fun. You really want to jump right in, but your bikini is in the bag that Niall's got. You grab a deckchair, pop your shades on, put the bag on the table next to you and relax in the warm sunshine.

Suddenly, there's a commotion, and five guys in swimming shorts run into the pool area and jump straight in, doing flips and whooping. They're splashing and diving under the water, but there's no question who they are. You're looking at all five members of One Direction. This holiday is going to be amazing if it carries on like this! Niall's over in the deep end of the pool, practising his diving. How are you going to get his attention?

If you decide:

1. To call to him as loudly as you can, go to **B1a**, on **page 43**.

2. To divebomb into the pool fully clothed, go to **B1b**, on **page 44**.

B2: It's almost lunchtime and your stomach starts to growl hungrily. The restaurant is painted in bright colours, and there are big vases of flowers on the tables. Everything on the menu looks delicious, and you grab a table and get ready to tuck into a tasty meal.

As you sip your tropical fruit juice, you notice a table in the corner. It looks like someone else is dining alone this lunch-time, and whoever it is has a very familiar-looking mop of blonde hair.

You peek around the side of a pot plant, just to be sure. Yep, it's Niall alright, and it looks like he's just about to demolish a huge plate of chicken. You know how much he loves his food, and you're not sure how he'll feel about having his lunch interrupted. What are you going to do?

If you decide:

1. To be bold and ask if you can join him for lunch, go to **B2a**, on **page 44**.

2. To ask the waiter to send over a chocolate sundae and tell Niall it's from you, go to **B2b**, on **page 45**.

B1a: Cupping your hands around your mouth, you let out a whoop that ends up turning into a sort of weird yodel. It is also very, very loud!

Niall pauses on the edge of the pool and stares at you with a curious look on his face. You gesture for him to come over and after a second or two he agrees.

You hold up the bag. 'Does this look familiar?'

Niall looks adorably confused. 'Wait ... how did you get this?' he asks.

'At the airport. You took mine by accident. Had you not noticed?'

'I hadn't even looked yet, we just got to our rooms and then came straight down here – Liam's been excited about hitting the waterslides for ages. That would have been really embarrassing later! Thanks so much for bringing it to me.'

He looks at his watch. 'We've got some time before we have to get ready for the show tonight. Why don't you stay and hang out with us? I'll go get your bag now.'

In a flash, you're reunited with your stuff and ready for the best pool party of your life.

THE END

B1b: It's only when you're in mid-air that you realize this could be a mistake! You land with an enormous splash, and when you surface, hair dripping wet, all five One Direction boys are staring at you with their mouths hanging open. You've often imagined getting their attention, but it's never been quite like this in your head!

Slowly, Louis starts to clap, and the other boys all join in. You take a bow as best you can when treading water in a swimming pool, and swim over to Niall.

You explain about the airport mix-up and point to his bag at the side of the pool.

Niall slaps his hand to his head. 'Phew! You really saved me there, and I think you deserve a reward – especially after making an entrance like that! How would you like to come to our show tonight?'

Your smile is so big you feel like it's going to jump right off your face. What a perfect start to your holiday!

THE END

B2a: Your heart is in your mouth as you make your way over to Niall's table, but his face lights up in a grin as you ask to sit and eat with him.

'Sure,' he says, motioning for you to sit down. 'I hate eating on my own anyway.'

The next hour passes in a blur. Niall makes you laugh so hard that juice comes out of your nose, and you even manage to convince him to share some of his chips with you. Result! By the end of the meal, you feel like you've known him for ages. As you swap the bags and are reunited with your stuff, Niall wraps his arms around you in a huge bear hug, and promises to hang out with you the next day. This holiday just keeps getting better!

THE END

B2b: As a giant sundae appears at Niall's table, his cry of delight echoes across the restaurant, and he looks around. His eyes meet yours, and you wave shyly. He grabs the sundae and comes over to your table, getting covered in chocolate sauce as he does so.

'I have been dreaming about an ice cream like this for ages! Thank you so much,' he says, beaming.

'How would you like it with a side order of your stuff?' you say, smiling and holding up his bag.

Niall looks so happy and relieved that, for a second, you think he's going to lean over the table and kiss you. Your heart starts beating like mad as he looks deep into your eyes. But then he calls to the waiter and asks for another spoon. Sharing an ice cream with a gorgeous dreamboat? That sounds like a fabulous afternoon to you!

THE END

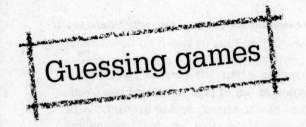

Guessing games

READ THE QUOTES FROM NIALL BELOW AND SEE IF YOU CAN WORK OUT WHO OR WHAT ON EARTH HE IS TALKING ABOUT. THERE ARE CLUES TO HELP YOU FIGURE IT OUT AND YOU CAN FIND THE ANSWERS ON **PAGE 93** IF YOU REALLY GET STUCK.

1. 'He's got this metabolism so he can pick what weight he wants to be. He's like a boxer!'

Clue: You wouldn't want to see this curly-haired cutie in the boxing ring.

Who is it? ....

2. 'I started all my lessons, and then we went on tour.'

Clue: Nialler doesn't need any more va va vroom as far as you're concerned.

What is it? ....

3. 'It's the only thing I do like about my body.'

Clue: You'd reassure Niall about his good looks in the blink of an eye.

What is it? ....

4. 'He's got this deadly headlock … Our tour manager always has to tell him to calm down on the headlock, because he could probably hurt someone!'

Clue: And you thought he was the sensible one.

Who is it? ....

5. 'We were all really good friends with her. We hadn't seen her for a while and then we saw her at the Radio 1 Teen Awards recently. She came into our dressing room and we talked to her for a while. I miss her actually. I love how cute she looks in her new video, but I don't fancy her.'

Clue: This girl's no brat and she's got real swagger.

Who is it? ....

6. 'I see it at literally the last second and I slap it down, otherwise it was going to break my collarbone!'

Clue: When Niall's on stage performing, this might not be the best way to get him to call you!

What is it? ....

7. 'I was first up on stage and she gave me a kiss. I didn't wash my face for about a week.'

Clue: Could Niall be living in a Teenage Dream?

Who is it? ....

8. 'That's what sickens me about this country. It cracks me up – I'm an Irishman!'

Clue: Nialler does get pretty thirsty when he's on tour in the USA.

What is it? ....

9. 'Zayn likes them, but I think they stink of really badly gone-off cheese.'

Clue: This Greek food might not be the best thing to put on Niall's pizza.

What is it? ....

10. 'I miss him, yeah, he's a cool character.'

Clue: This fellow Irishman might help decide if you've got the X Factor.

Who is it? ....

11. 'We were actually working for quite a lot of it, which was a bit upsetting.'

Clue: The 1D boys are hard at work, even on the most romantic day of the year.

What is it? ....

Spot the difference

Can you find eight differences between the top and bottom pictures?
You can check your answers on page 93.

Sweet tweets

JUST HOW CUTE CAN NIALLER BE IN ONLY 140 CHARACTERS?
READ SOME OF THE SUPER SWEET TWEETS FROM
@NIALLOFFICIAL TO FIND OUT.

Just went for dinner ! Italian food is off the chain!
Ridiculously good!

Ice packs ! Too much walking today! Knee is screamin'
at me! #lethimout

Rain is the last thing we needed today! Not good! Rain
rain go away.

Also massive thanks to everyone for birthday
messages and presents and cards! Much appreciated, last
year as a teen! Noooooo!

That wind was nuts yesterday! Got a cold now!
Electric blanket is gonna be on tonight!

Holy poo poo! Can't believe it! You guys have put us on
the top of the US charts with #TakeMeHome this week!

Meself and @zaynmalik are goin' for the pot noodle
and wotsits days again! love it.

Went to watch my boy @justinbieber tonight! Smashed
it! Great job dude! See ya soon

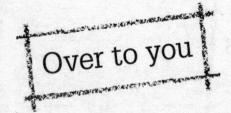

Over to you

IT'S TIME TO GET CREATIVE. USE THE NEXT THREE
PAGES TO WRITE YOUR ULTIMATE DAYDREAM ABOUT
NIALL. IF YOU'VE BEEN LUCKY ENOUGH TO SEE A 1D
SHOW IN REAL LIFE, IT COULD BE A REPORT OF THE
CONCERT, OR YOU COULD JUST LET YOUR IMAGINATION
RUN WILD AND CREATE YOUR PERFECT DAY. IF YOU'RE
STUCK, CHECK OUT THE BOX BELOW.

Need help getting started?
Try to include the answers to these questions:

- How would your day start?
- How long have you been a 1D fan?
- What do you love most about Niall?
- What are your favourite songs?
- Where would you take him?
- What would he wear?
- What would you eat together?
- What would you say to him?
- What would you want to ask him?
- What would you want him to ask you?
- How would your day end?

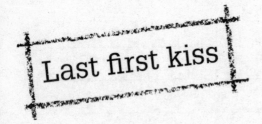

Last first kiss

IT'S TIME TO FIND OUT ABOUT NIALL'S ROMANTIC SIDE.
THESE QUOTES AND STORIES ABOUT THE IRISH CUTIE
ARE SURE TO LEAVE YOUR HEART ALL A-FLUTTER.

Niall once hired a boat for €15 and rowed his girlfriend
at the time across a lake while serenading her with his
soulful voice! Quite possibly the most romantic thing ever!
Some of his favourite songs to strum to are by Justin Bieber
and Jason Mraz.

Niall is a big fan of clever girls!

'I hate it when girls act stupid cos they think it's cute.
Intelligence is sexy.'

Niall thinks that not being in a relationship isn't,
necessarily, a bad thing. He explains:

'Being single doesn't mean you're weak, it means
you're strong enough to wait for what you deserve.'

Niall loves his downtime, but he's quick to put some
rumours about laziness to bed, and prove that romance is
still high on his list.

'All these things in the papers about me saying I'd rather sleep than find a girl is ridiculous. I was just explaining that on my time off I like to chill ... I'm not actually looking, but if the right girl came along, definitely.'

Niall's ex-girlfriend, Holly, opened up about Nialler's softer side.

'He was lovely – funny, cheeky and kind,' she said. 'He was also very affectionate – we always called each other "babe" and he'd always end his texts with a kiss.'

Niall isn't worried about playing the tough guy, and is honest about the connection he hopes to have with a girl.

'I'm an emotional guy, so I don't have to worry about a girl trying to get me to open up.'

He's a cutie, that's for sure, but for Nialler, his fans and the support they give him show true beauty. He said,

'The fans always tell me I'm beautiful, but no one will ever be as beautiful as them.'

Niall loves being a part of One Direction, but he does find that some of the pressures of life on the road make dating difficult.

'Travelling around the world and all the promo that we do – it doesn't leave time for a girlfriend. It really doesn't.'

Niall's looking forward to meeting the right person. He says his ideal girl would have green eyes, be cute, funny and chilled out, and not wear too much make-up.

Not only is Niall a hugely successful pop star, he can also cook, clean and do his own washing! According to his father, Bobby Horan, Niall has a soft and cuddly side, 'His mother taught him to bake ... he can do cupcakes.' His father added that his son will 'make someone a wonderful husband'. Swoon.

On stage at the MTV Video Music Awards, Niall got a kiss from superstar Katy Perry, which left him feeling more than a little lovesick.

'I don't think there will ever be anything cooler than kissing her ... until I marry her maybe!'

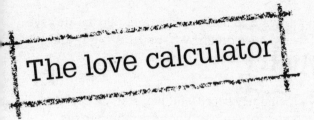

The love calculator

HERE'S A FAST AND FUN WAY TO WORK OUT WHETHER
YOU ARE NIALL'S PERFECT MATCH.

Write your name and his with 'LOVES' in the middle. Then
write down how many letter Ls, Os, Vs, Es and Ss there are
in both your names in a line – but don't include the ones in
the word 'love'. Add together pairs of numbers – the first
and the second, the second and the third and so on – to
work out a final 'percentage'. This tells you how likely you
are to be the one for Niall.

Here's an example:

HANNAH COHEN  NIALL HORAN

There are two Ls, two Os, zero Vs, one E and zero Ss.

Write this as: 2 2 0 1 0

Add together each pair of numbers until you have only
two left.

$$2\ 2\ 0\ 1\ 0$$
$$4\ 2\ 1\ 1$$
$$6\ 3\ 2$$
$$95\%$$

So stylish

NIALL MAY BE KNOWN FOR HIS CASUAL, LAID-BACK LOOK, BUT HE'S STILL SUPER STYLISH. RATE NIALL'S STYLE IN EACH OF HIS SIGNATURE LOOKS ON THE NEXT THREE PAGES BY USING THE STYLE-O-METER BELOW.

Style-O-Meter

★☆☆☆☆ Not a Fave

★★☆☆☆ Pretty Cool

★★★☆☆ Looking Good

★★★★☆ Love This Look

★★★★★ So Stylish!

At the very beginning ...

The first time he stepped out on stage in front of the
X Factor judges, Niall rocked a classic contemporary look.
He wore a navy blue T-shirt with a red, white and blue
checked shirt buttoned over the top. He paired this with
some loose denim jeans and cool navy suede trainers. What
do you make of Nialler's early fashion sense? Was it star
style or a rookie look?

What makes him beautiful

The video shoot for the band's first smash hit single took
place on a beach in the USA. Niall showed off his love for
casual chic, wearing a charcoal grey T-shirt, teamed with a
light-grey hooded jacket and stone-coloured chinos. Do you
rate this laid-back look for fun in the sun?

Perfect polos

The simple polo shirt is a Niall Horan style staple. He
seems to own one in every colour of the rainbow! Do you
prefer the feisty red, the classic grey, or the turquoise that
brings out his eyes? Decisions, decisions!

Style in black and white

For the boys' performance of 'Little Things' on the USA version of *The X Factor,* Niall looked chic and suave. With his blond hair slicked up in a quiff, Niall sported black trousers and a black T. He paired these with a loose black blazer with a white trim, giving his look an edgy, modern feel.

Rocking the red carpet

Several of the 1D boys claim that their night at the 2012 MTV Video Music Awards was the high point of their careers so far. The boys scooped three awards, and were dressed in their best when they attended the ceremony. Niall dared to be different and avoided the traditional shirt-and-tie look. He wore fitted black trousers with a button-down, rust-coloured sweater. What do you make of Niall's bold fashion move? Was it right for the red carpet?

A royal success

It's rare to see Niall in a dinner jacket, but when he wears it, he wears it well! Performing at the Royal Variety Performance, he wore smart black shoes, a black tuxedo and a crisp white shirt. Classic and drop dead gorgeous!

An Irish champion

The 1D boys were honoured to be asked to perform at
the closing ceremony of the Olympic Games in London.
Niall's look was at once casual and slick. He wore a pair of
pale blue jeans, with his trademark white trainers, and a
short-sleeved white shirt that showed off his summer tan.
Do you think this look deserves a gold medal?

A roller-coaster ride

Niall visited a theme park in the US and made the most of
some time off in the scorching heat. For his day out, Niall
looked relaxed and ready for some fun, wearing a white
logo T-shirt, grey knee-length shorts and trainers, with
some cool shades and a bright green baseball cap.

Cosy cover star

Niall graced the cover of *Teen Vogue* magazine, looking
every bit as polished and gorgeous as a top model. He
showed off a suave winter look, with tousled hair, a sea
green jumper in a chunky knit and a smart tan jacket
draped effortlessly over his shoulders. Is this a look you'd
like to see repeated, or is it a one-off wonder?

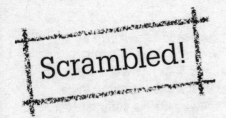

Scrambled!

THAT CHEEKY PRANKSTER LOUIS HAS MUDDLED UP THE NAMES OF ALL THE SONGS ON THE BAND'S SETLIST. CAN YOU HELP NIALL TO UNSCRAMBLE THEM BEFORE THE SHOW TONIGHT? THE ANSWERS ARE ON **PAGE 94**.

1. ISKS UYO

....

2. TELTIL GSIHNT

....

3. LELT EM A EIL

....

4. HSSE TNO RDFIAA

....

5. EVIL HEWLI REEW UGOYN

....

6. PU LAL GINTH

....

7. TEHAR KATCTA

....

8. NEO IHTNG

....

9. VERYHGNITE TOBUA UOY

....

10. CABK FRO UYO

....

11. HAWT SMEKA UYO FLABITEUU

....

12. UMRMSE VOLE

....

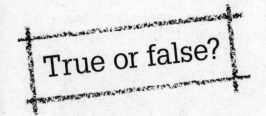

True or false?

READ THE STATEMENTS BELOW AND TICK WHETHER YOU THINK THEY ARE TRUE OR FALSE. YOU WILL GET AN EXTRA MARK IF YOU CAN GUESS WHICH OTHER BAND MEMBER THE FALSE ONES REFER TO. WRITE HIS NAME ON THE DOTTED LINE. THE ANSWERS ARE ON **PAGE 94**.

1. Niall once shaved his initials into Zayn's leg hair!

☐ True ☐ False. It was ....

2. For Christmas, Niall's friends bought him a revealing swimsuit called a 'Mankini'.

☐ True ☐ False. It was ....

3. In the video for the band's second smash hit single 'Gotta Be You', Niall gets a kiss from a gorgeous girl at the end.

☐ True ☐ False. It was ....

4. Niall's worst habit is that he farts all the time!

☐ True ☐ False. It is ....

5. During *The X Factor*'s boot camp stage of auditions, Niall sang a song by Oasis called 'Champagne Supernova'.

☐ True   ☐ False. It was ....

6. Niall has a tattoo of a sweet called an iced gem on his arm.

☐ True   ☐ False. It is ....

7. In Australia, Niall was given a piece of toast spread with Australian speciality Vegemite. He hated it so much that he had to spit it out on live TV!

☐ True   ☐ False. It was ....

8. Niall is the oldest member of One Direction.

☐ True   ☐ False. It is ....

Fact-tastic!

THERE'S NO DOUBT THAT YOU'RE A HUGE NIALL FAN,
BUT JUST HOW MUCH DO YOU KNOW ABOUT YOUR FAVE
1D LAD? READ THE FACTS BELOW AND PUT A TICK IN
THE BOXES NEXT TO THE ONES YOU ALREADY KNEW,
THEN CHECK OUT YOUR SUPER-FAN STATUS ON THE
SCORECARD ON **PAGE 68**.

☐ Niall's mum and dad split up when he was just five years old. He went to live with his dad.

☐ Niall, Liam and Harry had a joke played on them on TV channel Nickelodeon, when an actress, posing as a producer and wearing a fake baby bump, pretended to be giving birth in front of the boys. Louis and Zayn were in on the joke and could barely contain their laughter, while the other three boys panicked!

☐ For his 18th birthday, Niall's bandmates once bought him a life-sized statue of President Barack Obama, which he keeps on his balcony!

☐ When an American band claimed that they were called One Direction first, Niall joked that he and the other 1D boys would rename themselves Niall And The Potatoes.

☐ Niall's middle name is James.

☐ A good mate of Niall's is N-Dubz singer and *X Factor* judge Tulisa Contostavlos. When they hang out together they give themselves the nicknames Tom and Chez to confuse fans!

☐ Generous Niall bought his mum a car with some of his One Direction earnings.

☐ Niall's a big golf fan, and as well as organizing a charity golf game for his 19th birthday, he once offered to be the caddy (the person who carries the clubs) for Boyzone star Keith Duffy.

☐ Niall had white braces put on his teeth in 2011 to perfect his smile.

☐ All the One Direction boys share a wish to collaborate with Bruno Mars, but Niall admitted that he'd also love to get on stage and sing with rock legend Jon Bon Jovi.

☐ The band's schedule is so hectic that in 2011, poor Niall only managed to spend 30 days at home in Ireland.

☐ Talented Niall played acoustic and electric guitar on seven of the songs on the band's album *Take Me Home*.

☐ Niall says that his idea of a perfect first date would be taking a girl to a theme park, because it's fun and there's no chance for awkwardness.

When the boys were called back on stage after their heartbreaking rejections as soloists, they were all overjoyed to hear that they would be being put in a group together. Apparently, Niall was already thinking of the group's look and future. According to his bandmates, one of the first things Niall said when the new band was alone was, 'I think we should all dress like Louis, because I really like his shoes!'

SUPER-FAN SCORECARD

Score 0–4
You are a Niall newbie. There's still a lot of Niall knowledge that you have yet to master. Time to get studying!

Score 5–9
You're definitely a fan, but there's still more out there about Niall for you to find out about. Keep on going, and you'll soon be a true super-fan.

Score 10–14
You are a dedicated Directioner! You've really done your 1D homework and you're a proper Niall know-it-all.

Dare to dream

IF NIALL HADN'T FOLLOWED HIS DREAMS, THEN HE
NEVER WOULD HAVE LANDED HIMSELF A PLACE IN THE
HOTTEST BOY BAND ON THE PLANET. BUT THE IRISH
SWEETHEART HAS NOT LET FAME GO TO HIS HEAD.
HE REMAINS GROUNDED AND CARES DEEPLY FOR HIS
FAMILY, FRIENDS AND FANS.

Have a read of some of Niall's most inspirational quotes
below and dare to dream of what you could achieve if you
set your mind to it!

'I'm still in shock about how quickly everything has
happened ... And we're so excited about what's to come
in the future.'

What is your biggest dream for the future?

....

....

What are the steps you need to take to achieve your
dream?

....

....

'We always just remind ourselves how lucky we are to be in this position. It's what we've always dreamed of doing, so it's worth every early morning or late night.'

Do you think you would like to be famous?

....

What do you think are the best and worst things about being a celebrity?

....
....
....

'It's unbelievable how hectic our lives have got in a short time. I knew it would be busy, but I'm not sure I ever imagined it would get this busy this quickly. We don't complain though. We always just remind ourselves how lucky we are to be in this position.'

What's the hardest you've ever worked to achieve something you want?

....
....
....

Do you think it's luck, hard work or a bit of both that makes dreams come true?

....
....

'It makes a huge difference to be able to sing something that you've helped create.'

Do you think it's important that singers write their own songs?

....
....
....

If you were a songwriter, what would be your inspiration?

....
....
....

'We've been on TV shows and all sorts, and the more we do, the more we feel like we're getting stronger as a band.'

Would you prefer to be in the spotlight as a solo artist, or to have your friends around you?

....
....
....

If you were in Niall's position, and were put in a band with four strangers, how would you feel, and what would you do to bond?

....
....
....

'Obviously our everyday lives have changed, but I honestly can't see any of us ever getting big-headed or thinking we're special — there's too much banter between us for that to happen!'

If you were to become a megastar, what would you do to make sure you stayed grounded?

....
....
....

What would you miss most about everyday life if you were to become a celebrity?

....
....

'I want to go everywhere and do everything! And we want you to come along with us all the way.'

If you could travel anywhere in the world, where would you go and why?

....
....

'We have the most unbelievable fans.'

What would you do for your fans to show them you care?

....
....
....

Quickfire

YOU KNOW THAT YOU LOVE NIALLER, BUT DO YOU SOMETIMES STRUGGLE TO FIGURE OUT WHAT IT IS YOU LOVE THE MOST ABOUT HIM? IT'S TIME TO STOP THINKING AND START TICKING! READ EACH OF THE CHOICES BELOW, AND QUICKLY TICK THE OPTION THAT MOST APPEALS TO YOU.

Do you prefer ...

Niall's eyes? ⟷ His smile?

The way he sings? ⟷ The way he strums a guitar?

His gorgeous giggle? ⟷ His cute accent?

His sense of humour? ⟷ His sense of style?

His love for his fans? ⟷ His love for his family?

Super-fans

LIKE ALL THE 1D BOYS, NIALL IS SO GRATEFUL TO
EACH AND EVERY ONE OF HIS FANS FOR THE LOVE
AND SUPPORT THEY SHOW HIM. HOWEVER, THINGS
CAN SOMETIMES GET A LITTLE BIT CRAZY! READ THE
STORIES BELOW AND DECIDE IF THEY'RE TRUE OR FALSE.
THEN, CHECK OUT THE ANSWERS ON **PAGE 94**.

1. It's common knowledge that Louis receives lots of
carrots from adoring fans, after he said he likes girls
who eat carrots in an interview, but Niall has his own
veggie fan base, too. There's one group of girls who
appear at lots of the boys' shows, with potatoes for
him to sign!

☐ True Tale ☐ Fan Fake

2. It's not only Niall who sees his fans everywhere he
goes – his dad, Bobby, often has contact with them,
too. One Directioner came all the way from Canada
with her mum to see the house that Niall lived in. She
even asked to take photos of his bedroom!

☐ True Tale ☐ Fan Fake

3. When the boys are on stage performing, the excited crowd sometimes throws things on to the stage for them to keep. While Niall is quick to warn fans of the dangers of this (a flying object could hit one of the lads and would really hurt!) he did praise the originality of one fan who threw a walkie talkie on to the stage in the USA, while she kept the other one so she could talk to the boys. Genius!

☐ True Tale   ☐ Fan Fake

4. While in New York, Niall and Liam went out to get some food, but they hadn't bargained for the sheer number of devoted fans who wanted to accompany them. They were surrounded by screaming girls, and poor Niall admits to finding it a bit scary!

☐ True Tale   ☐ Fan Fake

5. Niall once opened his hotel-room door to find a large cardboard cut-out of a girl propped up in front of him. There was a note attached to it explaining that this was the best way the girl could think of to be close to Niall at all times. She added that she hoped he would take the cardboard version of her with him wherever he went.

☐ True Tale   ☐ Fan Fake

6. Niall revealed that the most dedicated (and bonkers) example of Directioner devotion was when a Swedish fan hid in a rubbish bin for several hours in a bid to meet her idols.

☐ True Tale   ☐ Fan Fake

A fabulous photoshoot

IMAGINE YOU ENTERED A COMPETITION TO SPEND
SOME TIME WITH ONE DIRECTION. FILL IN THE BLANKS
IN THIS FUN STORY TO MAKE IT UNIQUE. THERE ARE
SUGGESTIONS IN BRACKETS TO HELP YOU, OR YOU CAN
CHOOSE YOUR OWN WORDS TO USE. GET READY TO
GET CREATIVE!

It's been three days since you heard the radio
announcement about the 1D contest, and you've been
scribbling away ever since. The contest is to design a
One Direction poster, and show it off outside the station
when the lads come in for an interview. They will pick
their faves, and those lucky girls will get to take part in a
photoshoot for a glossy mag with One Direction!

You've been hard at work on your poster. It's for Niall
– your fave of the 1D boys. You want to make sure it's really

.... (bright/ original/ funny)
and covered in the things Niall loves. So far you've found a
picture of an Irish flag, the logo from his favourite

.... (football team/ restaurant)
plus some of the funniest quotes from the man himself.

You've just got to add lots of ....
(glitter/ stickers/ sequins) and then it's ready to go!

The finished poster looks great, and you're feeling pretty pleased with yourself as you take your place outside the radio station with the other hopeful 1D fans, all holding their own posters. Suddenly, a black car pulls up and there they are! Louis, Liam, Harry, Zayn and Niall jump out the car one by one, and the screams are deafening.

Niall looks gorgeous. He's wearing a ....
(shirt/ polo shirt/ jumper) that really brings out his eyes, with jeans and a cap. The boys walk up towards the entrance to the radio station, and you can see them smiling and pointing at some of the other posters in the crowd. You call out Niall's name and he turns and catches your eye. His eyes light up when he sees your poster and you almost melt

when he gives you a ....
(smile/ wink/ thumbs up)

The boys head inside, and you wait anxiously for the announcment of the winners. There are speakers set up outside so you can hear what's going on. The boys start

the interview with a .... (joke/ song/ game) and then it's time for the results. Harry's up first and he's

selected a huge sign with ....
(hearts/ lights/ stars) all over it, while Louis has gone for one that's a really realistic picture of him in his trademark stripes. Zayn chooses an artistic black-and-white number, and Liam's picked the poster that the girl next to you has

done. You give her a quick .... (hug/ high five) as she's taken to join the other winners. Then it's Niall's turn. Your heart is in your mouth as he starts speaking.

'I loved the colourful poster with the ....

on it,' he's saying. 'The girl who made it has .... (your hair colour) hair and she's wearing a dress with a

.... (polka dot/ bird/ flower) **pattern.'**

OMG! He's talking about you! You step forward and someone ushers you towards a sleek, black limo. You're going to be whisked away to a top-secret location for a glam makeover before your photoshoot with the boys. The limo is so cool – it's got tinted windows, and a box of

.... (tasty sweets/ cosmetics/ DVDs) for you and the other winners to enjoy. The others are all really nice. You can't quite believe the day you're about to have, and during the journey you have great fun

.... (getting to know each other/ singing along to One Direction songs/ talking about your fave 1D guys)

The car pulls up outside a cool-looking salon and you all bundle out of the limo and inside, where a team of stylists are waiting for you. The next two hours are a blur, but it's so much fun!

First, you get your hair styled. You choose to have it

.... (straightened/ coloured/ pinned up), and you love how cool it looks when it's all shiny and finished. Then it's over to the manicure station, where you pick a pretty polish to paint on your nails.

Finally, a stylist shows you a rail of gorgeous clothes, and together you pick an outfit for the shoot. You think that a

.... (preppy/ relaxed/ bohemian) style would be fun to try out, and the stylist helps you

select a .... (dress/ pair of jeans/ shirt),

and a beautiful ....
(necklace/ headband/ bracelet) to wear.

You're all set! With butterflies in your stomach, you get in the lift with the other winners, who are all looking lovely, and hit the button for the penthouse floor. This is where the photoshoot will be happening. Your heart is fluttering in

your chest, and as the door opens you feel ....
(excited/ happy/ nervous)

The boys are sitting on sofas and beanbags, and there's an

amazing view over the town. 'Hi,' says Niall, '.......................

....' (you look lovely/ your poster was great/ it's nice to meet you) You sit on the sofa with him and start chatting, while the photographer gets snapping. Niall is just as amazing as you thought he would be, and soon you feel like you've known him forever.

The others seem to be having a great time, too. Louis is

.... (cracking jokes/ doing a silly dance/ doing impressions) and making everyone laugh, and when Zayn suggests a game of Twister, things get very competitive! You don't want this day to end.

When the sun finally sets, Niall ....
(gives you a hug/ kisses you on the cheek/ squeezes your hand) and the other 1D boys wave you off. You feel as if you're walking on air – this has been such a great day!

A month later, the new edition of *Fab!* mag hits the shelves, and there you are, smiling next to Niall! The photos are amazing, but it's the memories that you'll treasure forever.

NIALL HAS SHOT TO SUPERSTARDOM IN RECORD TIME, BUT CAN YOU COMPLETE THE TIMELINE TO HIS SUCCESS? TAKE A LOOK AT THESE MAJOR MOMENTS IN HIS LIFE, AND SEE IF YOU CAN FILL IN THE BLANKS USING THE WORDS OR DATES FROM **PAGE 83**. CHECK YOUR ANSWERS ON **PAGE 94**.

.................................(1): Niall James Horan is born.

2003: Niall gets his first taste of the thrill of being on stage, when he plays the lead in ....(2) at his school.

2009: Niall performs in a local talent contest called *Stars In Their Eyes*, singing ....(3) by Jason Mraz. He does really well and appears in the paper.

May 2010: Niall plucks up the courage to audition for *The X Factor*, singing 'So Sick' by Ne-Yo in front of Simon Cowell, Louis Walsh, Cheryl Cole and guest judge ....(4).

September 2010: The judges decide to put One Direction together as a group, and the boys fly to Simon Cowell's house in ....(5), Spain, for the final round of auditions.

October 2010: Niall gets to meet his musical hero

..........................(6) while on *The X Factor*. Niall later said 'He's an absolute genius, and when he heard that I was a massive fan he came over to me and introduced himself. I was freaking out!'

..........................(7): One Direction perform in *The X Factor* live final, coming third in the competition behind Matt Cardle and Rebecca Ferguson. Niall was gutted to be leaving the competition, but Simon Cowell announced that *The X Factor* was 'just the beginning for these boys'.

March 2011: Niall and the rest of the band release their first book, *One Direction: Forever Young*, which climbs to the top of the bestseller list.

August 2011: One Direction's debut single

....(8) gets its first play on BBC Radio 1.

September 2011: Their debut single smashes straight in at No. 1 in the UK Top 40 and it goes on to spend

..................(9) consecutive weeks in the charts.

October 2011: Niall and the band film the video for their second single in ....(10), New York, and Niall can be seen playing guitar in some shots.

..........................(11): One Direction win Best British Single at the Brit Awards for their debut track 'What Makes You Beautiful'. 'Thank you so much to everyone who voted for us,' said an emotional Niall when collecting the award with the rest of the boys. 'Our fans are absolutely incredible, and this is one for you,' he said, holding the award up proudly.

March 2012: One Direction become the first British group in history to go straight to No. 1 in the US Billboard 200 chart with their album ....(12).

April 2012: One Direction arrive in ....(13) for their mini-tour of Australia and New Zealand.

May 2012: 'What Makes You Beautiful' goes double platinum in the US. The boys celebrate being one of the most successful British boy bands to make it in America.

August 2012: Niall and the lads have the honour of performing at the closing ceremony of the Olympic Games in ....(14).

August 2012: One Direction announce that their second album will be called ....(15).

September 2012: Niall and the boys film a TV advert for popular soft drink ....(16) in New Orleans, alongside American football star Drew Brees. In the advert, Niall tells Drew that if he hands over the can of drink, he can be in the band!

September 2012: One Direction triumph at the MTV Video Music Awards in Los Angeles, winning three prizes. They beat superstar artists including their good friend

....(17) to win Best Pop Video, Best New Artists and Most Share-worthy Video awards. Niall feels particularly star-struck when he collects an award from Katy Perry and she kisses him on the lips!

November 2012: Niall buys JLS singer ....'s (18) former pad in London.

November 2012: One Direction score a double chart success in the UK chart with both their album *Take Me Home* and their single ....(19) reaching the No. 1 spot.

January 2013: One Direction win two awards at The People's Choice Awards in Los Angeles, winning both Favourite Song and ....(20).

January 2013: Niall becomes the third member of the band to pass his driving test.

February 2013: One Direction embark on their world tour.

............................(21): A 3D film featuring the band is to be released across the globe, directed by the American filmmaker Morgan Spurlock. Niall shows off his movie-making skills by getting behind the camera during filming.

Missing words

Pepsi	Favourite Album
Oliver!	February 2012
August 2013	August 2013
London	'I'm Yours'
Marvin Humes	Michael Bublé
Justin Bieber	Katy Perry
13th September 1993	'Little Things'
Sydney	'What Makes You Beautiful'
Marbella	December 2010
Take Me Home	*Up All Night*
19	Lake Placid

What's your Niall style?

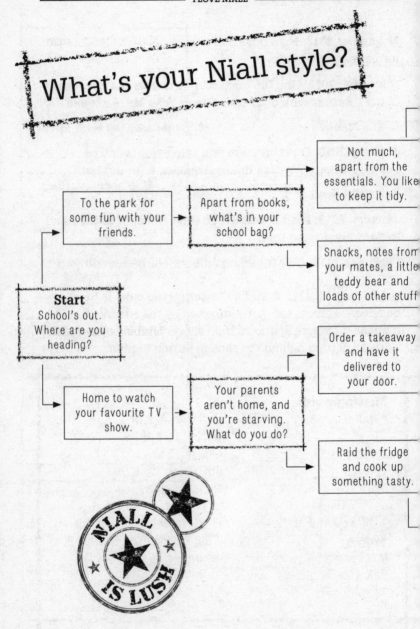

Start
School's out. Where are you heading?

To the park for some fun with your friends.

Home to watch your favourite TV show.

Apart from books, what's in your school bag?

Your parents aren't home, and you're starving. What do you do?

Not much, apart from the essentials. You like to keep it tidy.

Snacks, notes from your mates, a little teddy bear and loads of other stuff.

Order a takeaway and have it delivered to your door.

Raid the fridge and cook up something tasty.

NIALL IS LUSH

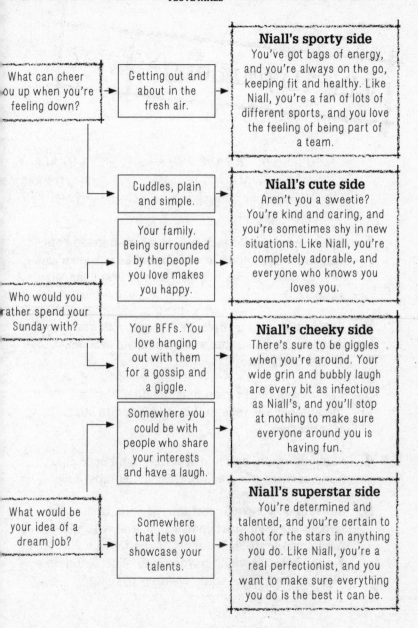

What can cheer you up when you're feeling down?

Getting out and about in the fresh air.

Niall's sporty side
You've got bags of energy, and you're always on the go, keeping fit and healthy. Like Niall, you're a fan of lots of different sports, and you love the feeling of being part of a team.

Cuddles, plain and simple.

Your family. Being surrounded by the people you love makes you happy.

Niall's cute side
Aren't you a sweetie? You're kind and caring, and you're sometimes shy in new situations. Like Niall, you're completely adorable, and everyone who knows you loves you.

Who would you rather spend your Sunday with?

Your BFFs. You love hanging out with them for a gossip and a giggle.

Somewhere you could be with people who share your interests and have a laugh.

Niall's cheeky side
There's sure to be giggles when you're around. Your wide grin and bubbly laugh are every bit as infectious as Niall's, and you'll stop at nothing to make sure everyone around you is having fun.

What would be your idea of a dream job?

Somewhere that lets you showcase your talents.

Niall's superstar side
You're determined and talented, and you're certain to shoot for the stars in anything you do. Like Niall, you're a real perfectionist, and you want to make sure everything you do is the best it can be.

The 1D challenge

GRAB A COUPLE OF FRIENDS AND A DICE, AND GET READY TO PLAY THIS ONE DIRECTION GAME. IT'S SURE TO HAVE YOU ALL IN FITS OF LAUGHTER! HERE'S HOW TO PLAY:

1. Each player should pick two numbers between one and six, and should write their names in the spaces next to their chosen numbers on the first chart on **page 87**.

2. Decide who will go first. That player rolls the dice. The number she rolls represents the player who must take up the challenge.

3. The chosen player then rolls the dice. Match the number she rolls to the song listed in chart number two.

4. She rolls again, and matches that number to chart number three, then again, for chart number four.

5. She will now have to perform the song from chart two, in the style from chart three, and with the extras from chart four! For example, if she rolled a 2, then a 4, then a 3, she would have to sing 'One Thing' in a high-pitched voice, while wearing pyjamas!

1.
PLAYERS' NAMES

1. _____
2. _____
3. _____
4. _____
5. _____
6. _____

2.
SONG TITLES

1. 'Kiss You'
2. 'One Thing'
3. 'Little Things'
4. 'Gotta Be You'
5. 'More Than This'
6. 'Back For You'

3.
SINGING STYLE

1. Backwards
2. Slow motion
3. Mime
4. High pitched
5. American accent
6. Whispering

4.
EXTRAS

1. Without smiling
2. While dancing a jig
3. Wearing pyjamas
4. With your mouth full
5. Hopping on one leg
6. Pretending to be a frog

Headline news

BEING A GLOBAL SUPERSTAR MEANS YOU'RE ALWAYS IN THE PUBLIC EYE — AND OFTEN IN THE NEWS. READ THE NEWS STORIES BELOW AND DECIDE IF THEY'RE BASED ON FACT, OR IF THEY'RE JUST RUMOURS. YOU CAN CHECK THE ANSWERS ON **PAGE 95**.

'INK-REDIBLE!'

He may have been the last of the lads to jump on the tattooing craze, but it appears that Niall, too, has got himself inked. Fans won't be able to gaze on the Irish cutie's body art, however, as Niall's chosen to get the shamrock design on his bum! Ouch!

☐ True News   ☐ Big fat fake

'FENDER BENDER'

Fans around the world were left worried when it was reported that the 1D boys had been in a car accident. A car drove into the back of their tour bus after a show in Birmingham, UK. Thankfully, none of the boys was hurt, and Niall even managed to laugh about it later that evening.

☐ True News   ☐ Big fat fake

'HE'S NO CHICKEN'

Niall's love of food has led him to branch out in his career. As well as continuing on his superstar journey with One Direction, he's opening a restaurant! The gourmet eaterie will specialize in spicy chicken and delicious pizzas, which the 1D boys love to eat. He's planning to name his new business venture 'Nialldo's' – catchy!

☐ True News   ☐ Big fat fake

'FAT FISH'

It seems that Niall tries to share his love of food with everyone and everything around him – even his pets! Unfortunately his two fish, Tom and Jerry, did not share Niall's appetite, and they sadly died from being overfed. What a fishy fiasco!

☐ True News   ☐ Big fat fake

'SHOES WET THROUGH'

During the video shoot for 'Live While We're Young', Niall was not his stylist's favourite person! He was warned at the start of the shoot that there was only one pair of his shoes available, so he'd need to treat them with care. Jumping straight into a giant paddling pool fully clothed might not have been what she had in mind ...

☐ True News   ☐ Big fat fake

Order! Order!

RANK THESE 10 THINGS ABOUT NIALL IN ORDER FROM WHAT'S MOST IMPORTANT TO YOU AS A FAN (1), TO WHAT'S LEAST IMPORTANT (10). WHY NOT ASK A FRIEND TO DO THE SAME AND SEE HOW THEY COMPARE?

His love of sports

His amazing appetite

His solo in 'Kiss You'

His sweet tweets

His talent for impressions

His blue eyes

His love for his fans

His look in the 'Gotta Be You' video

His trademark stage jump

His humble attitude

Rate It!

1. ....

2. ....

3. ....

4. ....

5. ....

6. ....

7. ....

8. ....

9. ....

10. ....

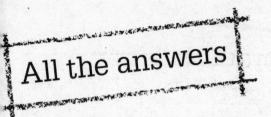

All the answers

Forever young
Pages 14–16

1.	b	**6.**	b
2.	a	**7.**	b
3.	c	**8.**	c
4.	b	**9.**	c
5.	a	**10.**	a

Cringe!
Pages 20–21

1.	True cringe	**5.**	Fake fail
2.	True cringe	**6.**	True cringe
3.	Fake fail	**7.**	Fake fail
4.	True cringe		

What was the question?
Pages 22–23

1.	C	**5.**	H
2.	F	**6.**	B
3.	I	**7.**	A
4.	K		

All directions!
Pages 24–25

L	L	E	W	O	C	N	O	M	I	S	L	B	W	T
L	P	A	Y	B	A	Z	S	T	I	A	L	O	U	K
A	Q	U	E	Z	Y	N	W	L	G	O	A	O	M	R
I	S	R	A	C	N	I	L	L	U	M	A	N	I	E
N	Y	A	Z	L	M	M	O	I	J	T	H	W	A	I
H	T	C	K	O	S	T	S	O	P	A	R	N	R	N
J	J	R	A	C	E	H	E	E	N	K	P	A	K	E
O	L	Y	D	I	A	C	R	R	Y	E	M	U	O	L
E	D	N	B	D	D	F	R	O	M	A	S	T	H
L	A	R	H	I	Q	N	I	K	W	E	L	I	A	M
N	H	H	T	A	K	L	U	P	A	H	Y	R	O	O
Y	G	A	R	O	C	L	P	E	E	O	C	T	B	E
N	O	R	U	S	H	A	T	H	E	M	H	S	I	M
O	X	R	W	A	B	P	T	U	P	E	T	L	L	O
Z	A	Y	B	M	O	U	L	E	X	T	A	L	E	O

Fab faves
Pages 29–31

1. b	**4.** a	**7.** b	**10.** b
2. c	**5.** a	**8.** c	**11.** c
3. b	**6.** c	**9.** a	**12.** b

Guessing games!
Pages 46–48

1. Harry Styles
2. Learning to drive
3. His eyes
4. Liam Payne
5. Cher Lloyd
6. A fan hrowing a phone on stage
7. Katy Perry
8. The drinking age in the USA
9. Olives
10. Louis Walsh
11. Valentine's Day

Spot the difference
In the picture section

1. Niall's sleeve has changed colour.
2. Zayn's jacket is missing a button.
3. Zayn's jacket is missing a pocket.
4. Liam has gold shoes.
5. Liam is rocking a bright green watch.
6. Harry has a red handkerchief.
7. Poor Harry's lost his watch in the bottom picture.
8. Louis has one longer sleeve in the bottom picture.

Scrambled!
Pages 62–63

1.	'Kiss You'	**7.**	'Heart Attack'
2.	'Little Things'	**8.**	'One Thing'
3.	'Tell Me A Lie'	**9.**	'Everything About You'
4.	'She's Not Afraid'	**10.**	'Back For You'
5.	'Live While We're Young'	**11.**	'What Makes You Beautiful'
6.	'Up All Night'	**12.**	'Summer Love'

True or false?
Pages 64–65

1.	False – it was Harry.	**5.**	True
2.	True	**6.**	False – it is Harry.
3.	False – it was Zayn.	**7.**	True
4.	True	**8.**	False – it is Louis.

Super-fans
Pages 74–75

1.	Fan Fake	**4.**	True Tale
2.	True Tale	**5.**	Fan Fake
3.	True Tale	**6.**	True Tale

Timeline
Pages 80–83

1.	13th September 1993	**4.**	Katy Perry
2.	Oliver!	**5.**	Marbella
3.	'I'm Yours'	**6.**	Michael Bublé

7. December 2010

8. 'What Makes You Beautiful'

9. 19

10. Lake Placid

11. February 2012

12. *Up All Night*

13. Sydney

14. London

15. *Take Me Home*

16. Pepsi

17. Justin Bieber

18. Marvin Humes

19. 'Little Things'

20. Favourite Album

21. August 2013

Headline news
Pages 88–89

'INK-REDIBLE!' – Big Fat Fake

'FENDER BENDER' – True News

'HE'S NO CHICKEN' – Big Fat Fake

'FAT FISH' – True News

'SHOES WET THROUGH' – True News

Also available ...

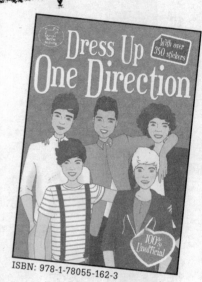

ISBN: 978-1-78055-162-3

ISBN: 978-1-78055-123-4

ISBN: 978-1-78243-013-1